A souvenir guide

Dyffryn Gardens

Vale of Glamorgan

C000179660

2

6

Exploring the Gardens 10
10 The Arboretum
12 Dyffryn House
14 The Vine Walk
14 The Lavender Court
15 The Paved Court
16 The Pompeian Garden
17 The Reflecting Pool
18 The Physic Garden
19 The Theatre Garden
20 The Cloisters
21 The Mediterranean Garden
22 The South Front
23 The Herbaceous Borders
24 The Walled Garden
26 The Glass House

The Gardens and House Today and into the Future 28

Community Links 32

Ymddiriedolaeth Genedlaethol
National Trust

'The grandest and most outstanding Edwardian gardens in Wales'

Dyffryn Gardens today have so much to offer at every level for all the family to enjoy. Take a walk through the Arboretum and wonder at the amazing collection of historic 'champion' trees that tower above you. Or explore the collection of themed outdoor 'garden rooms' of every conceivable design, each with its own distinctive style and planting. Enjoy the voluptuous Herbaceous Borders or study the rare and unusual plants and shrubs garnered from every corner of the globe.

But first (before delving into the detail) pause to take in the whole picture of this Grade I registered garden and relish the long view across the Great Lawns – a fitting setting for the imposing Grade II* house which was completely remodelled for the coal magnate John Cory in 1893.

Above The Great Lawn

Above The Herbaceous Borders

Right The gardens from the
north. The 'garden rooms' are to
the right of the Great Lawn; the
Arboretum to the left

'The gardens at Dyffryn are
the grandest and most
outstanding Edwardian
gardens in Wales. They are
comparable to some of the
most extravagant gardens
of the period in Britain.'

Register of Parks and Gardens of
Special Historic Interest in Wales

Grounded in history

While much of the design for Dyffryn House and Gardens as we see them today dates back just over a century, the story of the estate begins in the 7th century, when the then Manor of Worlton was given to Bishop Oudaceous of Llandaff. The first house was built in the 16th century by the Button family, who lived here for several generations. Indeed it's said that the ghost of Admiral Sir Thomas Button (c.1575–1634) still haunts the grounds.

The name was changed to Duffryn, St Nicholas in the 18th century, when the estate was sold to Thomas Pryce, whose home was the first to be known as Duffryn House. Features that date from this time include the pleasure grounds, the Walled Garden and the dipping pools. In 1891 the estate was sold to John Cory, who remodelled the house to create the grandiose Grade II* building we see today. The Cory family fortunes had been made in the South Wales coalmines and in shipping the coal across the world.

Thomas Mawson, a famous landscape architect of the time, produced the masterplan for the gardens (1903–4) and in 1906 began the massive task of realising these ambitious ideas.

But he did not do this alone. After John Cory's death in 1910, his third son Reginald collaborated on the design and continued to influence the gardens when his sister Florence was left the estate in trust. Reginald spent his life pursuing his passion for horticulture and plant hunting, which enabled him to gather the huge array of unusual plants in the gardens.

Changing times

The Cory family lived at Duffryn until Florence died in 1936, when it was purchased by Sir Cennydd Traherne, who in 1938 leased it to Glamorgan County Council. There followed a chequered period of institutional use, and the house has been closed since 1996, This was the time of Local Government reorganisation, and the Vale of Glamorgan Council stepped in to take on the property and bought the freehold. It was at this time that the name was changed to the correct Welsh version 'Dyffryn' (meaning valley).

Saved for the nation

In many ways it's a miracle that this estate has survived, but, with substantial support from the Heritage Lottery Fund, the true splendour of the house and gardens can now be enjoyed as one. Dyffryn has entered a new era in its history, as work continues on the restoration of the grand house with its fine rooms that reflect the status and aspirations of the wealthy Cory family. Today too, as the years of dedicated restoration by modern gardeners and volunteers come to fruition, we can see many of the unique features that the dynamic partnership of Cory and Mawson created.

And now that the National Trust has taken over the stewardship of this special place on a 50-year lease, there will be further opportunities to enjoy and be involved with Dyffryn in the way that John Cory – generous philanthropist that he was – would have wanted.

Opposite Admiral Sir Thomas Button, painted about 1610. His ghost is said to haunt the gardens

Right John Cory's good works are remembered by this statue in Gorsedd Gardens, Cardiff

History of the Gardens

Grand ambition

It's intriguing to understand the way in which the two enthusiasts, Thomas Mawson and Reginald Cory, approached the project at Dyffryn Gardens early in the 20th century. Mawson was already an eminent and well-established landscape architect, designing gardens at home and abroad. Although Reginald had read law at Cambridge, his real interest lay in horticulture and plant collecting. So this was a gift: the opportunity to focus all his experience and passion right here on his doorstep. Such collaboration could not fail to create a unique and stunning designed landscape.

Reginald Cory was an enthusiastic plant hunter, going on trips himself with Lawrence Johnston (of Hidcote Manor) and John Taylor to South Africa in 1927. He also sponsored expeditions by such leading plant collectors as George Forrest and H.F. Coomber.

Perfect partners

Mawson's own words sum up the admiration he felt for the man who soon became a close working partner in this grand ambition:

'Mr Reginald Cory is a typical example of the English enthusiast for horticulture and arboriculture at its best. He is a member of the council of the Royal Horticultural Society, a liveryman of the Ancient Guild of gardeners, a well-known writer on horticulture, and an experimenter whose researches have greatly enriched our store of knowledge in a vastly interesting field of human enterprise. His collection of conifers and ornamental and flowering shrubs has been brought together from every quarter of the globe.'

The Art and Craft of Garden Making, 1926

Above Reginald Cory

Left Thomas Mawson

Prized dahlias

Reginald Cory is probably most famous for his dahlia collection. With the help of his gardener Mr Cobb, a garden was created for Cory's large-scale dahlia trials of 1913 and 1914, in which 7,000 dahlias spanning 1,000 cultivars were tested.

In 1923 he established the Cory Cup, which is still annually awarded by the Royal Horticultural Society for the production of new hardy hybrids for the garden. He himself was presented with a gold medal by the Royal Horticultural Society and made president of the Dahlia Society.

Cory remained at Dyffryn until his marriage in 1930, when he moved to Wareham in Dorset. Sadly, he died four years later. He left bequests to institutions such as the Royal Horticultural Society, Lindley Library and the Cambridge University Botanic Garden. But perhaps his greatest legacy is the sheer variety of shrubs and trees from across the world and the imaginative design and plantings that we still enjoy here at Dyffryn Gardens.

Below The Physic Garden

Designing Dyffryn
The masterplan

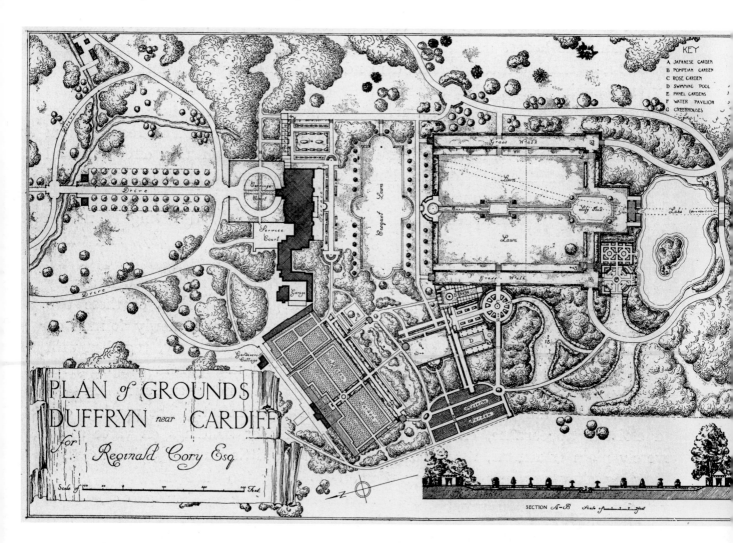

KEY
A JAPANESE GARDEN
B POMPEIAN GARDEN
C ROSE GARDEN
D SWIMMING POOL
E PANEL GARDENS
F WATER PAVILION
G GREENHOUSES

PLAN of GROUNDS
DUFFRYN near CARDIFF
for Reginald Cory Esq

SECTION A-B

We're fortunate that we have Mawson's masterplan (1903–4), as well as several chapters in various publications where he writes in detail about the gardens. We also have the beautiful paintings of the watercolourist Edith Adie, who was commissioned in the early 1920s by Reginald Cory to produce views of the gardens. They record the sheer abundance and riot of colour that was Dyffryn at the time.

Mawson was clear about what he had to do to complement John Cory's grand mansion. He determined 'to plan a great lawn extending from the old part of the garden on the south front, the object being to gain a sense of scale, a restful base to the house and a compensating expanse of view from the principal rooms to make up for the lack of more distant landscape views.'

The long central canal and the pond which held Cory's superb collection of water lilies were important, as Mawson said, in order to 'secure variety', while the long colourfully planted terrace bed on the south front and the huge fastigiate yews that still survive were used to emphasise the formality of this Edwardian garden.

Secret gardens

The extraordinary themed outdoor garden rooms leading from the Herbaceous Borders on the western side of the garden make Dyffryn different from Mawson's earlier work. Each had its own character of design and planting, and each was separated from its neighbour by arches, walls or hedges of clipped yew. They pre-date the better known examples at Hidcote Manor and Sissinghurst Castle and are on a grander scale.

As Mawson says, 'We felt at liberty to indulge in every phase of garden design which the site and my client's catholic views suggested.' He also recognised that there were startling contrasts, but noted, 'as each garden is enclosed in its own screen of architecture or foliage, it seldom clashed with its neighbour.'

These creations are another outcome of the partnership between Cory and Mawson, and several reflect the impact of their visit to Italy together. Surely the most spectacular is the Roman-styled Pompeian Garden, built in 1909 with its grand colonnades and loggias and a flowing fountain surrounded by a wisteria-draped pergola.

From across the world

The garden rooms at Dyffryn were designed to display Cory's huge array of 'ornamental and flowering shrubs … brought together from every quarter of the globe', as Mawson explained. So there were the Theatre Garden (which provided a fitting platform for Cory's display of bonsai), the Yew Walk, the Cloisters, the Lavender Court and the Rose or Topiary Garden. Cory appears to have masterminded the Bathing Pool Garden fringed with pink geraniums, as well as the Paved Court with its semi-circular dipping pond.

Mawson was determined that he would avoid creating 'an arboricultural museum' by weaving all the features into 'a cohesive whole'. Gazing across the complete landscape that is Dyffryn, we can see that he realised his ambition.

Opposite Mawson's masterplan for Dyffryn, as illustrated in his *The Art and Craft of Garden Making* (1926)

Below The Bathing Pool Garden in June 1923; watercolour by Edith Adie (RHS/Lindley Library)

Exploring the Gardens

The Arboretum

Rooted in history

The Arboretum is a true testament to the ambitions and vision of Reginald Cory. The area originally contained a native woodland and an open field section which Reginald used as his nursery area. Here he planted out many of the trees and shrubs that he'd brought back from expeditions to such far-flung places as China, South Africa and the West Indies. But, disrupted by the years of the First World War, these plantings matured and so became the Arboretum.

Mawson records that when he began his work in 1906 there was already an impressive display of mature trees and, indeed, several trees date back to the old pleasure grounds of

Opposite The Arboretum

Right The rockery by the
North Lawn in winter

Below The Fernery in July

the early 18th century. However, some of the fine and rare specimens now seen growing here were planted much more recently by successive head gardeners to produce the impressive collection we enjoy today.

Spot the champions

The Arboretum now boasts no fewer than 17 champion trees as well as many Welsh and county-status champions. This is no mere beauty contest: the champions are defined by the Tree Register of the British Isles which bases its classification on criteria such as girth and height as well as appearance.

Just stand and gaze in awe at the fastigiate hornbeam (*Carpinus betulus* 'Fastigiata'), with its fan of 65ft (20m) pole-like branches spreading over an entire glade, and the 39ft (12m) high paperbark maple (*Acer griseum*) towering above with its fat patterned trunk of flaking chestnut orange bark, grown from seed collected by the great plant hunter Ernest 'Chinese' Wilson in the early 1900s. Close by are many smaller paperbark maple trees which may well have come from the original planting and could, in time, become the champions of the future. Others include the Chinese elm (*Ulmus parvifolia*), of special interest for its use in bonsai, as well as thorns, pear trees, crab apples and the impressive southern cucumber tree (*Magnolia acuminata* var. *subcordata*).

The bigger picture

But there's much more to enjoy. Close to the paperbark maple is another stunning prostrate specimen of the maidenhair fern tree (*Ginkgo biloba*), which spreads its beautiful foliage close to the ground. The oak circle probably dates from the 18th or early 19th century, as does the impressive Lucombe oak to be found on the edge of the Arboretum on the archery lawn. Tread carefully around the hay meadows that offer an important habitat for a whole range of wildlife through the seasons.

And, just below the Arboretum, pause a moment to enjoy the Fernery and the Heather Gardens on the outcrops of exposed limestone.

The important trees are not just confined to the Arboretum. The West Garden has several fascinating examples of early introductions such as the Chinese wing nut (*Pterocarya stenoptera*), the swamp cypress (*Taxodium distichum*) and the Japanese white-flowering *Wisteria venusta*.

Truly today a garden for all seasons, the changing colours and profiles offer infinite variety across the entire landscape of Dyffryn Gardens.

Dyffryn House

'The Stately Pile'

It is the sum of the parts which makes Dyffryn a special place. A Grade II* listed building, the house is recognised for its exceptional interiors, but also for the importance of its setting within the Grade I registered garden. Mawson planned the gardens to complement the grand style of the house, of which he said: 'The design of the residence is reminiscent of an Italian villa as interpreted by English architects and may be described as a picturesque and even stately pile.'

Dyffryn House was one of the last great country houses built in Wales and reflects the tastes and aspirations of the dynamic and successful trading empire created by the Cory brothers, who were important figures in the history of south Wales.

When John Cory bought the estate in 1891, he commissioned a local Newport architect, E.A. Lansdowne, to remodel the Duffryn house built by Thomas Pryce in 1749, in order to create the mansion we see today. The design is a combination of French Renaissance

Above The north front of the house

and English Baroque with the principal rooms in the opulent style of the late Victorian period.

The house has faced an uncertain future since the Cory family left in 1936. Indeed, it's surprising that so many of its important features have survived. It was last used in 1996 for education conferences, and there's been no public access to the house since that time. But now, with the support of the Heritage Lottery Fund, the Vale of Glamorgan Council, Cadw and the National Trust, it's being restored to reveal some of the fine features of the opulent rooms within the house.

Left The south front on 24 August 1923; watercolour by Edith Adie (RHS/Lindley Library)

Below The south front

The Vine Walk
The Lavender Court

Above **The Vine Walk**

Left **Lavender Court**

The Paved Court

Right The Paved Court in
August–September 1923;
watercolour by Edith Adie
(RHS/Lindley Library)

Below The Paved Court

The Pompeian Garden

Above The Pompeian
Garden

Left The Pompeian Garden
in 1923; watercolour by
Edith Adie (RHS/Lindley
Library)

Opposite The Reflecting
Pool

The Reflecting
Pool

The Physic Garden

The Theatre Garden

Right A view from the
Cloisters to the Theatre
Garden

Below The Theatre
Garden

Opposite and left The
Physic Garden in July

The Cloisters

Above **Alliums** in the summer border

Left **The Cloisters**

The Mediterranean Garden

Right The Mediterranean
Garden

The South Front

The Herbaceous Borders

Above The Herbaceous
Borders in August 1922 or
1923; watercolour by Edith
Adie (RHS/Lindley Library)

Left The South Front

Right The Herbaceous
Borders

The Walled Garden

Plot to plate

Self-sufficiency was a high priority when Dyffryn was in its heyday. The fruit and vegetable gardens were already established when Mawson began his work. Indeed, they may date back to the 17th century, but his hand is very evident in the Walled Gardens as they evolved. Mawson worked in the Edwardian style and believed that kitchen gardens can and should be places of beauty, while continuing to supply the house with a whole range of flowers, fruit and vegetables.

Gladioli in the Walled Garden

Opposite below
Volunteers at work in the Walled Garden

In his book *The Art and Craft of Garden Making* Mawson devoted a whole chapter to the walled kitchen garden and another to vineries and glass houses:

'To the soul attuned to sympathy no pleasure exceeds being able to wander round a prim walled garden enjoying the fragrance of the blossom in spring and watching the setting of the fruit and its various developments through the successive seasons until the gathering in.'

This was not the mass-production style that became popular towards the end of the Arts and Crafts period and that we might expect today. The whole area for planting was only about one and a half acres, with a reserve garden set aside for some less attractive vegetables.

Today, Mawson's ideas of fruit walls and espaliers lining the paths have been incorporated into the lower garden, together with the wiring of the west and east walls to grow apricots, plums and pears. By including herbaceous borders growing fresh-cut flowers for the house, the garden continues to be a thing of beauty. It is already producing plenty of succulent fruit and vegetables that are for sale at the Bothy at the side of the Walled Garden.

Two original dipping ponds, used for watering and washing plants, have been rediscovered by the archaeologists and have been reinstated, adding further to the design and structure of the garden.

Don't miss one other important addition. The spirit of Mr Thomas, the last Head Gardener at Dyffryn, lives on as a modern-day scarecrow that points us clearly to his Bothy. Here we find displays of artefacts which reflect the old labour-intensive ways of working when the gardens would have employed up to 40 gardeners.

The Glass House

People and glass houses

Moving through the Walled Garden, we see the impressive new Glass House which replaces the more recent structures that were condemned in the late 1990s. The original glass houses were used by Reginald Cory to provide a microclimate in which he could grow his exotic plants from all over the world. The new building now houses fascinating cacti and orchid collections which remain true to the Cory spirit.

The orchids are displayed much as they would have been in Reginald's day and include many examples from collections of his time including: *Miltonia spectabilis*, dating back to the early 19th century; the *Stanhopea tigrina*

from Llywelyn on the Penllegaer estate near Swansea; and many hybrids from the Veitch collection.

The whole impact of the cacti is of a dramatic, almost lunar landscape, with still rare and exotic species such as *Echinocactus grusonii* from Mexico, which is popularly known as golden barrel cactus or mother-in-law's cushion.

Cory himself went on a trip to South Africa, from where he brought back succulents for his own collection. He also collected cacti on a visit to America, but none of the original plants survives. Central to the present cactus display is the collection of plants grown in Stokesey, North Yorkshire, by Jack Voase. Sadly, he was no longer able to maintain his extensive range of plants, so new homes were needed in 2011. Fortunately, Dyffryn's new Glass House passed the test and now displays some of his most interesting specimens in a fine new setting.

The Gardens and House Today and into the Future

Growing forever

Looking at the gardens today it is difficult to realise the state of disrepair some parts had reached. But after substantial support from the Heritage Lottery Fund and the considerable efforts of staff and volunteers, the place again shows the splendour that Mawson and Cory had intended. Work to meticulously restore Mawson's original designs, particularly in the garden rooms, began in earnest in 1998.

Mawson had left ample detail about his vision for Dyffryn in his masterplan. Inexplicably, Reginald Cory requested that his papers at Dyffryn and at his residence in St James's, London, be burnt upon his death. Sadly, this appears to have included his records of his plantings, as none has yet been found. However, his dahlia trial information appeared in horticultural publications of the day, and such historical articles are proving to be key references in the planting restoration.

The Edith Adie watercolours provide a good colour guide for the modern-day interpreters of the garden, together with the fascinating black-and-white photographs taken by Nearne Roff and commissioned by Reginald Cory between 1910 and 1925.

Much of the restoration work in the gardens has focussed on the 'garden rooms', many of which now reflect the original designs. The Pompeian Garden has been extensively restored and is now a venue for civil marriage ceremonies.

Above Volunteers weeding the borders below the south front

Opposite A vine undergoes close inspection

Great expectations

So the passion and the spirit of the enthusiasts who created Dyffryn Gardens live on. The gardens have been lovingly and expertly restored by specialist contractors and the modern gardeners, ably supported by nearly a hundred volunteers. And there is much more to come as the new plantings mature and additional innovative ideas develop.

Work continues on the 100ft (30m) long Herbaceous Borders, originally called the Italian Terrace. The south-facing terraces are already full of colour and contrast, just as they were in the 1920s. The arches covered with rambling roses contrast with the brighter hues of the phlox, the yellow helianthus and the orange of the campus vine.

Cory's importance to the Dahlia Society will be recognised in the plans for Dyffryn. Where appropriate, plants which have won the annual Cory Cup, awarded by the Royal Horticultural Society and started by Reginald, will be woven into the existing planting schemes.

The Theatre Garden, once the stage for Cory's bonsai collection, is now one of Dyffryn's performance venues, providing a superb setting for outdoor presentations of music and theatre.

Mawson's original plans for the lake below the Great Lawn seem to have survived for only a few years, probably because it flooded cellars in the house. Now a children's maze is mown annually into the lawn area, and there are further plans to provide other facilities for families to enjoy.

One significant change will be the development of a winter garden in place of the Australasian Garden, developed more recently by successive head gardeners. Its protected microclimate will provide the perfect enclosed environment for a scented winter garden with level access.

So the work continues. The opportunities to share ideas with other leading gardens such as Hidcote Manor and Sissinghurst will surely bear fruit and bring yet another dimension to Dyffryn Gardens.

Other features have changed. The Bathing Pool Garden, where the Cory family swimming pool had been filled in and grassed over in 1974, has been restored to a more shallow reflecting pool. Watch carefully and quietly here, and you may discover the rare great crested newts breeding in the water in the summer. Dyffryn is also home to a number of bat species, including the lesser horseshoe.

Other schemes included the restoration of the Lavender Court, planting a selection of heritage roses for display in the Rose Garden, and developing the medicinal plant collections in the Physic Garden.

In 2000 the gardens were designated a Grade I registered garden. Part of the designation states: 'The structure of the gardens, combining the expansively formal and the intricately intimate, survives almost in its entirety, with some modifications within the general framework. Within the gardens are many notable trees, including some very early introductions'.

Grand rooms revived

And now we're finally realising the long-held ambition to bring the two elements of Dyffryn back together as they were originally designed. Once again, we'll be able to get a real sense of the grandeur and the lavish life-style of the period when the Corys lived at Dyffryn. We can also begin to appreciate the incredible skills of the craftsmen and specialist conservators who have worked here.

The restoration has focused on the grand principal rooms on the east side of the house, where the Cory family would have spent most of their time, and the master bedroom on the first floor.

The Tudor-style Great Hall with its oak panelling is a reminder that Dyffryn was once the centre of an ancient manor. The impressive stained glass window shows Queen Elizabeth I at Tilbury.

The elaborate marble and alabaster fireplaces are a special feature of the house. The Blue and Red Drawing Rooms have matching 17th-century fireplaces brought in by John Cory from Scarsdale House, the home of the Curzon family. Closer scrutiny reveals that one depicts peace – the other war. The fine silk wall hangings have been restored and the flamboyant ceiling paintings include work by the artist T.W. Hay.

Other rooms will celebrate the family, their role in the industrial story of South Wales, and how their passions for plant collecting and plant breeding were funded by this wealth.

Rooms on the upper floor provide the perfect vantage point from which to appreciate the designed gardens and to enjoy the stunning views and vistas that have been created.

Left Fireplace in the Great Hall

It's the ideal place to find out more about Mawson's masterplan for the garden and the plant hunters who gathered so many of the exotic plants and trees that we still see at Dyffryn today.

There will also be further opportunities to bring more of the house into use for the benefit of people of all ages and the communities who have played an important role in its history.

Below Queen Elizabeth I at Tilbury. Stained glass in the Great Hall

Right Painted ceiling in the Red Drawing Room

Community Links

Going local

The Cory family was renowned for its philanthropy and its generosity towards social, educational and moral reform causes in Cardiff. In memory of his work, a bronze statue of John Cory was erected in the city. The inscription reads: 'John Cory, Coal Owner, Philanthropist. This statue is erected by his friends and fellow citizens as a token of their appreciation of his world wide sympathies 1906.'

This approach was continued by Sir Cennydd G. Traherne, who bought the Dyffryn Estate after the death of the Corys and later leased the house and gardens to Glamorgan County Council on condition that it should be used for 'public education and enjoyment'. Traherne also was a founder member and president of the Friends of Dyffryn Gardens, which was established in 1983.

The natural assets of the estate continue to be enjoyed in myriad ways. Taking advantage of the dark skies around the property, an Observatory for Cardiff Astronomical Society has recently been opened at Dyffryn. A partnership has been developed with the Cardiff Vale and Valleys Beekeepers Association, resulting in the re-introduction of beehives and a crop of Dyffryn honey, which is sold in the gift shop.

In the early part of the 20th century Reginald Cory set up an experimental fruit farm, run, as Mawson described, 'on scientific principles on which almost every known variety of apples, pears, plums, and cherries has been tested'. Sadly, the orchard was removed many decades ago. Now there are plans to work with local people to set up a new heritage orchard on fields outside the gardens to grow many of the species trialled by Cory.

So the partnerships continue, through community involvement and social enterprise. With a significant proportion of the population of Wales on its doorstep, Dyffryn really does offer the opportunity to 'go local' and encourage more support. Future plans include further opportunities for volunteers and trainees to learn new skills of garden restoration and an activity programme which will help to bring the history of this special place to life.

Above Statue of John Cory in Cardiff

Below Explaining the bee hives